Metamorphosis

By Cassie Veselovsky

Copyright 2022 Helen Veselovsky
All rights reserved

This book is about the metamorphosis, or transformation, of a caterpillar into a butterfly and can be sung to the tune of "The Wheels on the Bus"

The eggs are laid on the plants,

on the plants, on the plants.

The eggs are laid on the plants

by a butterfly.

Painted Jezabel butterfly laying eggs

The caterpillar hatches from the egg,
from the egg, from the egg.
The caterpillar hatches from the egg
very hungry.

White butterfly larvae and unhatched eggs on a cabbage leaf

The caterpillar crawls and eats, crawls and eats, crawls and eats. The caterpillar crawls and eats day after day.

A monarch caterpillar on a milkweed leaf

The caterpillar turns into a chrysalis,

a chrysalis, a chrysalis.

The caterpillar turns into a chrysalis

hidden in leaves.

The chrysalis of a monarch butterfly

The chrysalis begins to wiggle and shake, wiggle and shake, wiggle and shake.

The chrysalis begins to wiggle and shake protecting life inside.

A chrysalis has very little protection from predators.

If it senses danger, it will start to wiggle and shake to scare them off.

The butterfly finally breaks free

breaks free, breaks free.

The butterfly finally breaks free

from the chrysalis.

A newly transformed Red Helen Butterfly

Metamorphosis is the process in which an animal physically changes like a caterpillar into a butterfly. Metamorphosis happens in different types of animals such as insets, amphibians, and some aquatic creatures.

The process of going through metamorphosis is referred to as a life cycle and usually includes different stages: egg, larvae, pupa and adult. The pupa stage is only found in insects and and during that stage they may be enclosed in a structure like a nest, cocoon or shell.

On the next few pages we will take a look at the life cycle of other animals that go through metamorphosis.

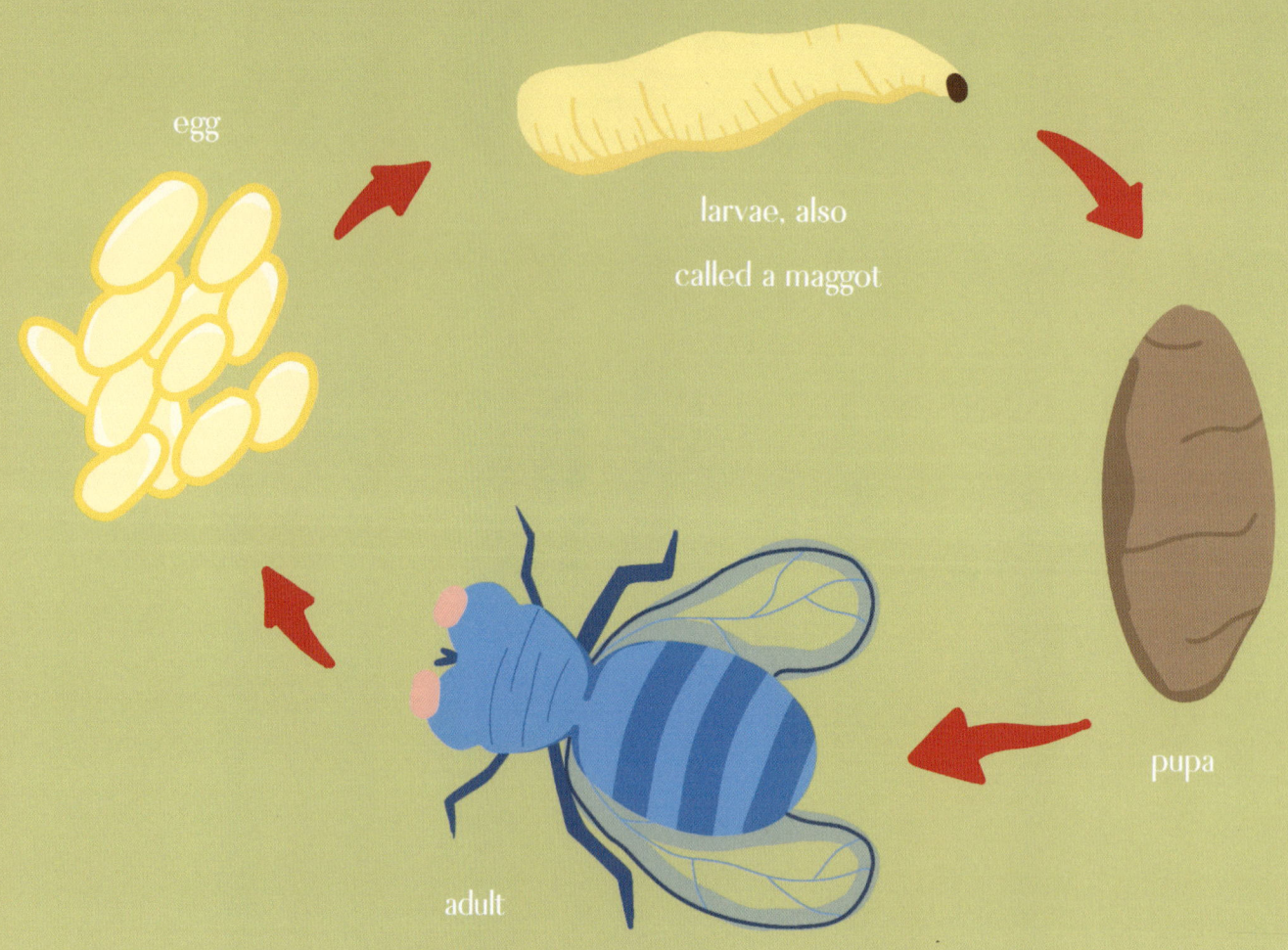

What Stage?

What Stage?

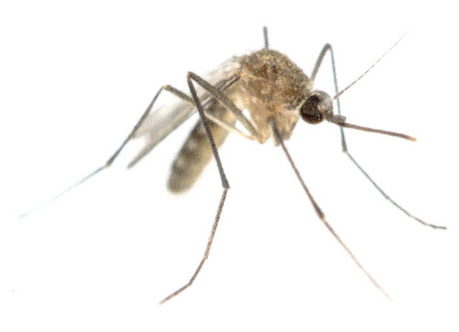

What Stage?

Answers:

larvae

adult

pupa

adult

larvae

egg

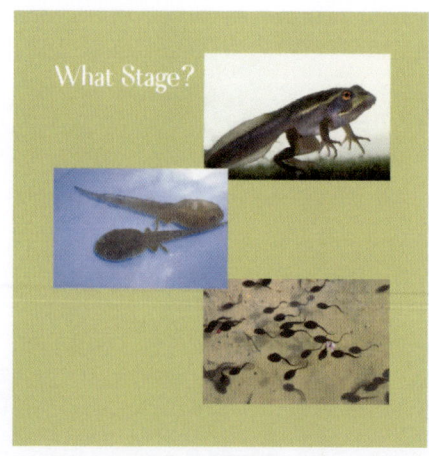

froglet

larvae

larvae

For more information about metamorphosis, check out your local library!

Cassie is passionate about early literacy and aims to create books that are fun and can be used as tools to help parents and kids. Check out some of the other interactive titles such as:

   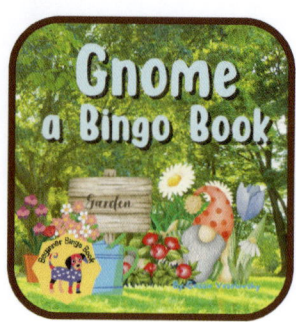

Where to find Cassie online:

- Amazon author page https://www.amazon.com/author/cassie_veselovsky
- Pinterest https://www.pinterest.com/im_a_librarian/
- Instagram https://www.instagram.com/im_a_librarian/
- TikTok https://www.tiktok.com/@im_a_librarian
- Blog https://lonecow.blogspot.com/